Tall Tales

poems by

Briahn Kelly-Brennan

Finishing Line Press
Georgetown, Kentucky

Tall Tales

To my beloved sister Margaret Rooney My guardian angel growing up
My best poetry buddy
and life's adventure partner

I love you sis

This is the most outrageously unique collection of poems you have ever met, eye to eye, way above all the other animals in your safari. It must be the vantage point of height that sees the world so differently, that tumbles out baby giraffes to get up on their own and begin their untoward journeys. Read on and marvel at how different the world is from this poet's amazing point of view. I plan to read and reread and stop only to graze on these luminous poems.

—**Fran Claggett-Holland**, teacher, poet, admirer of Briahn's mind

ACKNOWLEDGMENTS

Thank you Ruth Ark for your persistent love and support
Thank you Monday Poets for a safe place and amazing help and feedback
Thank you Fran Claggett-Holland for wonderful teachings and continued mentorship
Thank you all my readers for helping me feel seen and appreciated

Publisher: Leah Huete de Maines
Editor: Christen Kincaid
Cover Art: Briahn Kelly-Brennan
Author Photo: Margaret Rooney
Cover Design: Elizabeth Maines McCleavy

Order online: www.finishinglinepress.com
also available on amazon.com

Author inquiries and mail orders:
Finishing Line Press
PO Box 1626
Georgetown, Kentucky 40324
USA

Contents

The Big Bang

It's like as if a greyblue tornado picked up your house
pulled it up, roots and all, slammed it down and I
mean SLAMMED maybe even in the same spot but twisted
a little turned around not all the way say a quarter
turn so you get up in the sleepy morning and bump into the closet.

Each day you learn that things are the same but not
the same in just enough of a way that you think
—your body thinks—it knows and it almost really
does but not quite—not enough—so you just
miss everything a little to the left a little
to the right the light is so different anymore
and the breeze, the breeze you didn't even know
you knew suddenly feels wrong rustling
papers from a different direction. You try to make the change, try to get
used to the new world but it's just not right. It's just not right. I'm just not
right.

At least there is a breeze still the light shows colors in new
ways even new colors though with different angles if I go
slow—very slow—I can remember everything
is in a different place now and I am fine.
I am fine. The chickens haven't noticed
a thing the cats still hunt gophers in the early evenings there is
beauty there is light. There is a breeze.

Written

So the story goes
The good guys always win
It was meant to be
Though for a thousand years
Rice grew in these terraces

The good guys always win
They are heroes on the side of God
Though for a thousand years
Unmoved even by earthquakes
Mortarless the stone temple had stood

They were heroes on the side of God
Noble, even
Unmoved even by earthquakes
Like those 16th century sandstone buddhas
That they toppled in triumph

Noble, even
The hunter rode bareback, full gallop
Like those 16th century stone buddhas
Felled by foreign invaders
This time with disease in their gifts

Their hunters rode bareback, full gallop
They were meant to be
Felled by foreign invaders
So the story goes

Winning

They say the tortoise won
Really. The tortoise.
Steady, persistent, head down
Trudging the straight and narrow
Plodding the shortest distance
From beginning to end

And not the hare. The wild hare.
Skipping from place to place
Sniffing here, digging there
Run run run
Play play play
Bounce bounce bounce
Between beginning and end

What exactly
Did the tortoise
win?

How to Plant Seed Without Dreaming of Summer Tomatoes

I climbed a mountain once
More than once
More than one
To see the world differently

More than once
Eased down into thickening air
From seeing the world differently
And began to forget

Easing down into thick air
Moment by moment
I began to forget
I had to forget

To live in one moment
Not more than one
I must forget
I climbed a mountain once

MemoryBin II: Contents May Have Shifted

I remember
It wasn't the moon shouting its fullness
It was the ventriloquist sun
From behind its corner of earth
  your hands were cold and I stepped in front of you
  pulled your arms around me
  held your hands under my jacket, warming on my belly
  your head turned
  pressing your cheek into my shoulder
Yes, that was the day
I remember your hands, cold, in front of you
you wrapped your arms around me
in my warm jacket
under my belly
your cheek turned, pressed to my collar
  I remember the day well
  your cold hands under my warm belly
  I wrapped my heart around them
  your forehead pressed into my cheek
I won't ever forget that day
your hands were cold
we wrapped warm around each other
cheek to cheek
  I remember your hands
  that time we wrapped the warm day
  around us

Crow

for Fran Claggett-Holland

Maybe it's not that hard, Crow
maybe I can just say
I am afraid
(Bow twice, present to us
the shiny objects of your discernments
that we dazzle into verse under your spell)

The pull of your mate
already gone, thin as air
across your wings
(you circle, feather, and spread
tuck a little something
into each opening mind)

Her meaning in your world
ruffles memories
like a voice
(we hold you
with the small warm strings
of our poems)

Too soon will come the day
when these anchors
are no match
for the wind

Linda Loveland Reid Does Not Fit into a Poem
For Linda

An artist writer director event host
art lecturer
mother of three
notorious praise-ducker
cheerfully herding us all
toward community
Her life "a place where perfect
could happen at any moment"

Gads!
Who IS this woman?

"You are what you ART"
she claims
Ha!
A clue

She describes her watercolors
"Gentle, yet can be assertive with a mind of its own."

The "earthiness and rich depth" of oils
carries her paintings of complex spirited women
in casual poses
unhurried and present

Evolving into acrylic abstracts
"untethered from a reference point"
vivid and adventurous
full of movement

So, is she what she arts?
Yeah
She's all that

Quotes from Linda

Sister

For Margaret

She's reading
Focused as a frog on a fly
Brilliant as the beginning of time
Willing to enter another's moment

Solid like the North Pole
She bends light and beads years
Stopping to illuminate
the one molecule that matters

Down the Habit Hole

There once was a hole in the ground
I always tried to go 'round
Though I oft turned away
At the end of the day
We ALL knew where I could be found

Grace

When you throw all
Your bits and ends
Into the pot
And the soup
Tastes good

Soup

Splash splash dinkle dinkle, dunkle dunkle dunkle,
glug glug glug glug
Umph. Clunk. Scratch scratch fwoooooosh
Slice slice knife slice twice slice slice, thrice slice slice slice
knife slice knife slice slice
Chop chop, chop it chop it chop, chop it chop
chop it up, chop it up, chop it chop it, chop
Scrape slide slide schuss slide schuss, sizzle hiss hiss spit, sizzle hiss hiss
sizzle spit hiss hiss, hiss sizzle spit

Spatu-la flip flip spatua-la flap, spatu-lee spatu-la spatu-laha ha
ha, ha ha ha ha haaaa, spatu-lee spatu-la spatu-lum
Tong plop tong plop tong plop, slide scrape splash
tickety tickety tickety tickety, tickety tickety tap tap tap
slurp. more salt
sprink... sprink... sprink...
tickety tickety tickety, tickety tickety tickety, tickety tickety tap tap

Ladle oh ladle oh ladle ladle ladle oh, ladle oh ladle oh, oh ladle ladle oh
tink slurp tink slurp tink slurp , tear dunk chew chew, tear dunk chew
tink slurp slurp tink tink tink slurp tear wipe chew tear wipe chew
ahhhhh

What it is

It's alarming
How many times I wake
Myself with noises
I didn't know
A nose could make

It's timing
How with a stir and shake
So many ingredients
I didn't know
Were in a cake

It's raining
So many autumn signs and still
I didn't know
I had to rake

It's enlightening
How many times in different ways
I often make the same mistake
I didn't know
What's at stake

I Find Myself

I find myself laughing
Voices from the picnic
Mimic a chorus of crickets
Afternoons always sound so warm

Voices from some picnic
Waves of leaves rustle a breeze
The warm sounds of afternoon
In the slow light of a low hanging sun

Leaves rustle the breeze
A mirage of flat-foot frogs
In the slow hanging light
I start to slip under its wake

Flat-foot frogs mirror
A picnic of mimicking crickets
I wake with a start
To find myself laughing

Slow Drift of an Untethered Mind on a Sunny Afternoon

A thought appears
A sudden memory
Some shooting star
Extinguishing all others

A memory
Its randomness
Extinguishing all others
Your face in profile

Its randomness
That small telling gesture
Your face
As I knew it

That small telling gesture
Unconscious in its revelations
I knew it
Something passed between us

In its revelations
Something was understood, settled
Passed between us
Though really nothing happened

Something was settled
As if nothing happened
And really nothing happened
But what was that

As if nothing
Some shooting thought
But what is that
A star appears

A Thumb at Arm's Length

the sky darkens and darkens
the yellow circle falls to the ground
light breaks into small sharp points
above
around
three elongate
disappear

dark increases small sounds
one sound slides up then down
then two then the thousand ups and downs
over
under
each other
in pulses

a new light
no bigger than a thumb at arm's length
comes
up
from the flat edge of earth
a deeper tone begins
lifts in echoes
loud then quiet

and as thumb-light rises into a movement of dark shapes
slapping
air
faint at first, then loud
louder loudest then diminished
as they move across the light

I too fall into darkness
darkness different than the lack of light behind my eyes
movement of images I know
now in different motion
where there is no gravity
sequence is meaningless

but I know from times before now
like the many times before
I will be
may be
pulled
up
yet again
by that roundness
that one
that hurts my eyes to look at
yet brings me so thoroughly
here

Plunge

Mind like water
Muted and slow
Sensing vibrations
A memory before words
Twist and turn like the fish
We came from

Released from earth's weight
Feel the body
As we remember it
Held by water's soft persistence
Twist and turn like the fish
We used to be

Breathe in deep
Blow out slow
The world expands
To here to now
The need to find meaning
Dissolves
Twist and turn like the fish
You are

A pool The ocean
A blue tiled shower
Reminders
In my one wavy ribboning life

To Plunge

Mice at Night

The windy night is swinging light
All along the hall
The woodstove's bright to fight cold's bite
Outlines stalk the wall

The cat becomes a lion
The mouse is two feet tall

The door squeaks high as mice sneak by
Low in the glow of the flame
In the line of sight, if the timing's right
The hunger among us seeks prey

And the fire begins to roar
As the lion walks away

Fish Shticks

They come in like surfing
All shiny in yellow and red
Flashing their tail fins
None of them turn their head
Instead
In a block paddle straight to the rocks
They nibble and peck, nobody talks
Then they ride the next wave
Back into a little cave

The filtering daylight
Ribboning down from the top
Makes everything half-night
Right up until the drop
Then plop
It is so fine they are all inclined
To slide out of sight where no-one can find
A single sea thing
In the darkness depths can bring

Down in this churning
Deep in the sea-weedy kelp
Fishlets are learning
To be on their own—no help
A whelp
Has to flow in and out like a pro
Dodging long fronds wherever it goes
And it goes all around
Making underwater sounds

Up at the topside
Whelps joining in to the slip
Roll with a high tide
One of them shifts a hip
Then flip
A hundred turn, swing out right on cue
None of them miss, it's just what fish do
'Cause you know that all fish
Are well schooled

Day Long Strut Song
(chorus in italics)

Barking out a quick quack
Crowing to the peck pack
Hopping from her sit site
Chasing down a bit bite
A bit bite

Hey Chicken Chicken
Eat Another Bug

Pecking at a slug snag
Stooping for a grub grab
Snacking in the dill dell
'Til she has her fill full
Her fill full

Hey Chicken Chicken
Eat Another Bug

Strutting with a flip flap
Dozing in a snap nap
Jumping on a stump step
Poking with a pick peck
A pick peck

Hey Chicken Chicken
Eat Another Bug

Following the sun signs
Homing to her pin pine
Slowing when the sun's done
Roosting with her hen hon
A bit bite
Her fill full
A pick peck
Her hen hon

Hey Chicken Chicken
Eat Another Bug

Eight Degrees of Carrot

I.   The pull of the nearing moon quickens the sprout

II.   Green sprawl boosted skyward as
      Marrow wedges underground
      Stretching itself into existence

III. Uptaking traces of glacier, fossil, volcano
      Limestone sweetened, strong from sedimental seabeds

IV.   Banking on the soil's sense of humus
      Decomposed from a millennium of memories

V.   A planet turns
      The carrot widens
      Mycelium networks the news, seducing squatters:
      Dark brown snout beetles, six-spotted leaf hoppers
      Red-headed slender fly on yellow legs, shiny-black

VI.   Lighter than a kiting spider
      Dew forms drops on carrot tops
      Watering the frogs

VII. Sunrays fill and fill a rabble of buds to overflowering
      Feeding enlightenment to the flighty

VIII. Telos springs from umbel origins
      Diving the breeze in pike position
      Lands in a pawprint of soil
      Tuned to the moon

CatWalk

crushed scent prowls up her paws, curves away in green spirals
crouched below that swoop of sky lifted by mists, watching
yellow black stripes mine each ripe flower
swift lemon-itchy insect feet
sweet sweet sweet

thrumming brindle grass, bitter and soft in waves, opens
for the secret fur nose to sniff at chickens marching,
wingtips tucked behind, weight this way
then that, one eye forward to look
chook chook chook

Consumed

Desire as big as the valley
When flat orange light hounds the horizon
In the reckless shadows of coyote brush
Through the timid clatter of reedgrass
Among manzanita's hasty leaves
Here here here and now

The purring of untame teeth
Orange light hounds the horizon
Through timid clatters of reedgrass
An endless feral seeking

A soft bit of grey or brown
In the reckless shadows of coyote brush
Among manzanita's hasty leaves
Behind between beneath

Desire as big as the valley
Here here here and now
The purring of untame teeth
An endless feral seeking
That soft bit of grey or brown
Behind between beneath

Millennia

Because the earth
Moved mountains
White egrets drink
Pure fallen water
From this cup
Of rock

Ice

Today comes up cold
Melts blue
All over the afternoon
Where white bears walk
On hard hard water

At Sacramento Wildlife Refuge

Ten thousand cranes lift as one
Dizzying the sky
Like fish

Shastina

A river bends and unbends, scattering light
On the way to briny waters
Following turns of earth's rough surface
Carving out its own shape
Long before the simmering cone will lift sky's blue edge
The river coursing draws life to its elemental sound

A crater rises, magma gathers, a widening rush of sound
Erupts the volcano's hot liquid light
Dredging a canyon from the western edge
Time, over a windfall of seed and water
Pours a forest along its shape
Rain fills the pocked surface

Pines bristle as breezes surface
Birds, with their arcs of sound
Move through trees according to their shape
Empty-boned, feather-light
Hearing food smelling water
Dive to the pond's forested edges

A frog, squatting at mud's uncertain edge,
Tastes air from the moving surface
Reflections shift in rumpled water
An absence of sound
In oblong patterns of dusty light
Signals the presence of danger, swift by its shape

The frog, a still and stealthy shape
Watches the shallow's greening edge
Midges blink in and out of striped light
Striders skitter the surface
A hollowed log fattening the roundfull sound
Of mating calls from across the waters

Tadpoles scatter in algae under water
Small darting tapered shapes
Drop blunt dampened sounds
Hunt the uneven edge
Sharp pecks wrinkle the surface
Nipping at bugs that alight

The settling sun drains the final light
From water's witnessing surface
Its round soundless shape falls over day's slow edge.

Strange

How wave behavior
changes
when you re-
arrange the water
There is no danger
it's just that

River water's drawn
through eddies and pools
where salmon spawn
Over logs and rocks
the water rolls on
it's shape hold strong
There's nothing wrong
the wave stays in place
as the water moves along.

The ocean likes to shift
at a different pace
Lulls fish here
and back—lacks haste.
Buffleheads between the peaks
leaving wakes
In this case
it's the wave that moves along—
while the water stays in place.

Doran Beach

Winds riff sand into folds
Small shorebirds nestle in the dunes
Twisted cypress interrupt the wind
That blows into fog

Twisted cypress interrupt the wind
Wind that fetches distant waves
Blows into fog
Early morning slips the tide away

Wind fetches waves
Unsettling driftwood in spurts and rolls
Early morning slips away
Crabs crawl slideways in the wash

Driftwood spurts and rolls
Southward currents heap knobs of shell and tangle
Crabs crawl tidewise
Large brown birds parallel morning skies, orange pouches slack

Southward currents heap knobs and tangle
Bourne in bitter kelp forests holding fast in deeper waters
Large brown birds parallel morning skies
Circling wing shadows stir the fish

Born in bitter kelp forests holding fast
Flashy half-grown rockfish lull in shifting curves of green
Circling shadows stir
Seaweed loops and turns

Half-grown rockfish lull in briny curves
Past smells of wet sand, beyond foam of breaking waves
Seaweed loops and turns
Beaks hunt the churn, black ducks clatter lines of dark water

Past smells of wet sand, beyond breaking waves
Slack water marks the changing tide
Black ducks clack in dark water
Particles of light murmuring the surface turn to waves

Slack water marks the change
Drifting south in zig zag currents
Particles of light murmur the surface
Small white birds with angled wings dive

Drifting south in zig zags
Salt air bows the rasping call of gulls
Small white birds dive
Rowdy furrows of ebbing sea

Salt air bows the call of gulls
Skinny-beaked rummagers skitter
Rowdy ebbing furrows
Muddling the sand

Skinny-beaked skitterers rummage
Tending the fractal shore
Muddling the sand
Long-leg birds chase water's rogue edge

Tending the shore
Beach Hopper bubbles pock the wake
Quickstep birds chase water's edge
Sun bends orange light over the ocean

Bubbles pock the wake
Winds fold sand
Sun bends orange light
A shorebird
Nestles the dunes

All Along the Serious Day

Moods moving like clouds
or wanderings of the unplanted
Sun floats in its shell of sky
five naked ladies
turn pink at the sight
despite the urgent explanation of the leaves

When four frogs under an upturned bucket sing "La Donna E Mobile"
a rabbit in a black leather jacket will enter your dreams
and we will drink a book a day
as sylvan sounds
rub the bowl of your ear
until it rings
until it sings
until it opens